WHAT IF...

by JOSEPH M. FOX

PRICE/STERN/SLOAN

Publishers, Inc., Los Angeles

1979

WHAT IF

This is not a "reading" book, it is a "working" book, a "writing" book. Questions are designed to make you think— to evaluate yourself, your life, your ideals, your actions. Space is provided for you to record your responses.

The answers to some of the WHAT IFs will be very personal, so treat them with the care you would give your diary.

You must let yourself go in order to get into WHAT IF... For example, "If you are to have one more meal anywhere in the world, what and where would you eat?" Now you can't start thinking, "Why is this my last meal?" or "What happens to me after the meal?" You must either blot out such logical questions or answer them with pleasant suppositions.

IF you can let your imagination soar freely, even wildly, and IF you are willing to define yourself by the choices you make, then WHAT IF is for you!

WHAT IF...

1... you were a multi-millionaire, how would you spend your time?

2... you had to drive across the United States from coast to coast, or cross the Pacific Ocean on a small ship as a passenger, and you could choose only ONE companion, who would you ask?

✓ 3... you're stranded 50 miles from home and your car's engine blows up. Your family is out of the country and there are no rental cars, taxis or other transportation available, who would you call to come and get you?

4... you were to live in a cave for the rest of your life and you could pick one companion to spend the remaining time with, who would you choose?

WHAT IF...

✓ 5... you could give one -- and only one -- trait
to a friend, what trait would you give him/her?

✓ 6... you could tour any manufacturing plant in the
world, what would you tour?

✓ 7... you could, without fuss or bother, change your
name, first, last or both, every record and the
world would now know you by your new name,
would you change your name; if so, to what
and why?

8... you were about to enter a lottery for a new
name and had the power to reject a drawn
name, what name would you refuse to accept?

WHAT IF...

9... you could change any part of your body, would you?

Which part?

10... you could keep one part unchanged, which part?

11... you could become anyone in the world, would you do so? If your answer is yes, who would you choose to be; who would you not be?

12... you could live your life as a comic strip character or TV character, who would you choose to be?

WHAT IF...

13... you could go back in time and be anyone you wished to be, who would you be?
(ASSUME that you MUST do this)

Who would you not be?

14... you had to publicly select the accomplishment of your life, what would you pick?

15... you could be any sports hero (of today or of the past), who would you be?

16... you could have one superhuman power, what would you select?

WHAT IF...

✓**17...** you had to spend the rest of your life in one building -- you're loaded with money -- what building would you choose?

✓**18...** you could unravel one of the world's great mysteries, which would you choose?

✓**19...** you had to leave the city in which you live (if you don't live in a city, just keep going) and you could live in any city in the world, where would you live?

✓**20...** you had just learned to read and could select one and only one book to read, what would you choose?

WHAT IF...

21... you could see only one movie in your life, which would you see?

22... you were to have one more meal and then go to the great beyond where you didn't get any food, what would you eat and where?

23... you could have one more drink before it was over, what would you drink?

24... you could drink only ONE liquid for the rest of your life, what would you drink ?

WHAT IF...

 25... you had to eat the same meal for the
rest of your life -- no substitutes-- every
meal the same for the next 20-40 years,
what would you eat?

26... you could have dinner with one movie
star, at his or her prime, who would you
choose?

✓ 27... you could spend one hour with anyone
in the world today, who would that be?

✓ 28... you could spend one day with one historical
person, with whom would you spend that day
and why?

WHAT IF...

✓ **29...** you could bring someone from the past into today and give that person a tour of anything in the world, who would you bring and what would you show?

✓ **30...** you could spend two hours with any author of any time, who would you choose?

31... you were God and decided to eliminate ONE SERIOUS problem in the world today, what would that be?

32... you could wave a wand and eliminate one element (animal, vegetable, mineral) in the world today, just for the effect, what would that be? (This is for fun, so how about: doorknobs, lawyers, television, toll booths...)

WHAT IF...

√33... a wave of your hand could forever banish one word from the language, what word would you choose?

34... you could keep one great mistake (your choice) of history from happening, which would you prevent?

35... you were God and decided to eliminate one set of people -- wipe them from the earth -- which people would go? *Wicked*

36... you could assure that one great invention or discovery of the last 100 years was to be invented -- that is, it is 1880 and you control future inventions -- If you don't assure its invention, it will not get invented, what would you invent (discover)?

WHAT IF...

✓ 37... you had to name the LEAST important invention of the last 100 years, what would it be?

38... you had to complete the following sentence, what would that experience be?

✓   The last experience I would want to have is:

39... one year after your death you could put a 20 word sentence into the mouth of your closest friend, what words would you choose?

40... you had to select only one adjective that describes you, what would that be?

WHAT IF...

41... you had to select the adjective that absolutely does not describe you, what would that be ?

42... the world were going to end in 10 minutes, what would you do?

43... the world were going to end in 24 hours, what would you do?

44... you knew the world were going to end in 30 days, what would you do? In what order? Would you tell anyone that it was going to end? Whom?

WHAT IF...

45... you knew the world were going to end in one year, what would you do? Would you tell anyone? Whom?

46... you were going to die in 10 minutes --- everyone else lives on -- what would you do? You were healthy for that time. Would you tell anyone? Whom?

47... you were going to die in one hour -- everyone else lives on -- what would you do?

48... you were going to die in 30 days, what would you do?

WHAT IF...

49... you were going to die in one year, what would you do?

50... you were in the hospital, had one day to live and were feeling pretty good (ignore the logic), who would you like to visit you?

51... you had one more sight to see, what would you choose?

52... you had one more thrill in store for your-self, what would you choose?

WHAT IF...

53... the world were about to end and you could go to one amusement, what would you choose?

54... you were to die in one hour and all you could do for that hour was to read comics, which comics would you read? Daily, Sunday and comic books are available.

55... you knew the world were going to end in two hours and all you could do was play one sport, what sport would you play?

56... the world were going to end in one hour and all you could do was watch one TV show, what would you watch? You may select any past or present show.

WHAT IF...

57... you had to watch one TV show every night for the rest of your life, which would you select?

58... you could take one show off the air, which show would you take off?

59... you were given three hours of prime time on TV to create your own show, what kind of show would you produce?

60... you deliberately put together a mismatched double feature, what two movies would you put together?

WHAT IF...

61... you were going to die in 30 minutes and all you could do was listen to one comedian, who would you listen to?

62... you were to taste the same taste from this moment on for the rest of your life, what taste would you pick?

63... the world were going to end in three hours and all you could do was read a book, what would you read? (I know you wouldn't want to read, but you must!)

64... you knew the world were going to end in three hours and you could see one stage play, what would you see?

WHAT IF...

65... you had five minutes before you passed on and could either relive one five-minute segment of your life, or live your last five minutes as they come, would you relive a segment; if so, what would it be?

66... you could relive your entire life and change ONE five-minute segment -- which, of course, could change the ensuing years -- would you change a five-minute segment and if so, what would that be?

67... you could relive your entire life, with no change, would you?

68... you could wipe away -- as though it was never said -- one statement you made in your life, would you do so? If so, which one?

WHAT IF...

69... you were to go through life again, with the same parents, in the same location, at the same time, what would you do differently?

70... you had a choice, after you die, would you want to be reborn and live another life?

71... you were about to be reborn -- in the year and place you choose -- would you want to be born male or female?

72... you were about to be reborn, in what country would you want to be born?

WHAT IF...

73... you had to be reborn as a plant, what plant would you choose to be?

74... you had to be reborn as an animal, what animal would you choose to be?

75... you had to be reborn during a famous historical period, what period would you choose?

76... heaven could hold only ten people and you could select them, who would you have join you in heaven and why?

WHAT IF...

77... you were, by chance, to run into a person from your past, someone you haven't seen for years, who would you want to run into?

Who would you not want to run into?

78... you were killed in an accident today, who would cry -- really cry -- for you?

79... you could have any job in the world, what would you choose ?

WHAT IF...

80... you could refuse any job in the world, what would you turn down ?

81... you were having a dinner party and could invite any five historical figures, who would you invite ?

82... you had to play a game every day for the rest of your life, what game would you choose ?